Question to Ponder

Have you ever thought about what your dog was thinking? Why did she or he choose to do this or that? Well, I am here to tell you about my dog, Nikki. She is stubborn and self-centered. I, at times, wonder what she is thinking. Is she talking to me at the same time? What message is she trying to convey to me?

Introduction to Author

Hello, my name is Dain Taylor. I am an educator, you tube creator, and writer. I am known as Mr. Tay Tay on you tube, and I specialize in writing and publishing books, developing curriculum, making videos, and making learning engaging and meaningful.

My seventh-grade language arts teacher, Mrs. Moreland, always made writing so much fun. I still recall writing a lot of journal entries for her. Bishop Corlis Dees II and Datha have always encouraged me to enjoy the journey in my Christian walk with the Lord and to make a plan. Pastor Seth and Libby have instilled the belief to trust in the Lord and to not give in to fear.

I would like to thank all of my readers. You are the reason why I write. I thank you for taking the opportunity to open and read this book and to take a journey with me into my world.

This is a work of nonfiction. Names, characters, places, and incidents are products of what happens in the author's daily life at home. Any resemblance to actual persons, living or dead, events, or locales is entirely coincidental.

Copyright © 2020 by Dain Taylor

All rights reserved. No part of this book may be reproduced or used in any manner without written permission of the copyright owner except for the use of quotations in a book review. For more information, address: daintylr@gmail.com

ISBN: 9781734900637 (paperback)-small version

Nikki's World: The Dog Walk

Written by Dain Taylor

Illustrated by Dain Taylor, Shanae Dees, and Diane Taylor

Published by Dain Taylor

Dedication Page

I would like to dedicate this book to our family dog, Nikki. Though she is kind of spoiled, she is a superhero. She has always been there to cheer up my mom, my dad, and me whenever we feel down. One time my mother fell, and Nikki assisted her up from the floor. My mom always says that she is my shadow.

Me: "From midnight on, you're always on my case."

Nikki: "What are you talking about, Master?"

Me: "I am talking about being the center of attention and taking up my bed space."

Nikki: *"How would you like to sleep in a cage all night? It is rough."*

Me: "What the heck! What are you doing? That happens to be my bed where you're drooling!"

Nikki: "You say that it's your bed!"

Nikki: "Well, I don't see your name written on it, Master."

Me: "Well, at least you're sleeping quiet, just like a mouse."

"For when you awaken up in the morning, you tear up the whole house."

Nikki: "What bed mattress can I tear up today?"

Nikki: *"I know the master left his sheet off the bed; it's chewing time!"*

Me: "What's your problem, dog? What could it be?"

Me: "Maybe, you just have to go outside and go pee!"

Nikki: *"Dude, you don't say!"*

Nikki: "Master, since we are in the house again, I want to play with my toys, and then go on a dog walk!"

Me: "Well, we're back inside? Where are you going? Your playroom!"

Me: "What could you possibly have on your mind?"

Nikki: *"Toys, dog walk, toys, dog walk, toys, unicorn, dog walk, unicorn! Where in the world is my unicorn?"*

Nikki: *"Now you are talking my language!"*

Me: "We can play with the unicorn, the old socks, and other toys, but please be on guard when playing with the girls and boys."

Nikki: "What are you talking about, Master?"

Nikki: "I am always gentle around the lads and gals."

Me: "Well, remember what happened to the mattress? You tend to get aggressive, and you tend to get so wild! I must remember Nikki that you're only a puppy child."

Nikki: "I am not a child anymore; I am thirty-five in dog years."

Nikkie: "Oh, that! It was Atlas, the cat, that made all of those holes."

Me: "Well, maybe it wasn't you. Maybe it was Atlas?"

Me: "Well, I don't know. It is around noon, and you, Nikki, keep following me throughout the house."

"What do you want me to do? Build a doghouse?"

Nikki: "No! I would like to have a mansion for me and my peeps: Hope and Eva."

Me: "This cannot be the answer as surely as any dog trainer can see."

Nikki: "Don't even think about sending me to another dog obedience school again! That lady gave me nightmares. She made me sit way too long."

Me: For you prefer to live inside and sleep right beside me."

Nikki: "I need to get you trained in 'Train-Your-Dog 101'."

Me: "Oh! I see that you are at the door!"

Nikki: "Train-your-dog rule #1: Go to the door to let your master know you need a walk!"

Me: "Can you bark me the answer or give me a clue?"

Nikkie: *"I don't speak human; I bark common sense."*

Me: "The answer is coming in perfect view."

Nikki: "Exhibit A, we have a door. Let's go outside of the door. You might want to get the leash!"

Me: "A walk! A walk! A walk is what you request! Please obey and do your best. Keep away from the paperboy and all the neighbors, too."

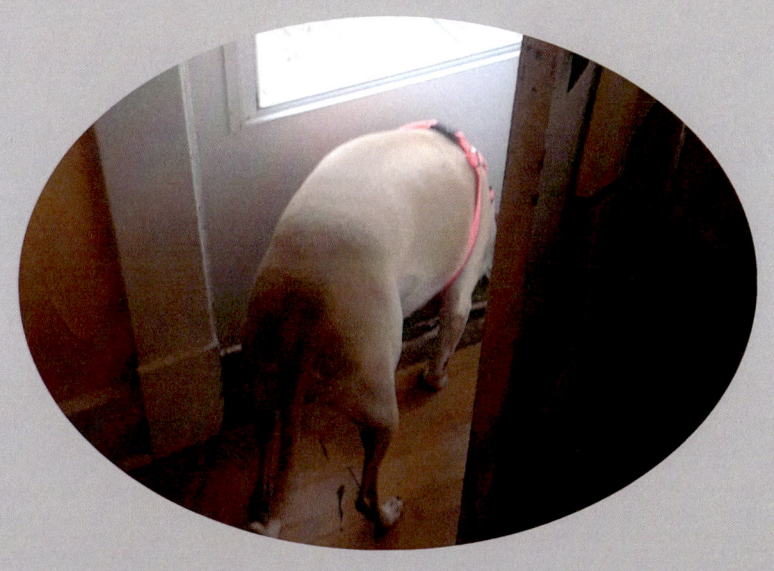

Nikki: "Ugh, Master, can you please finish with the rules already?"

Me: "I'm bringing the pooper scooper to pick up a turd or a few."

Nikki: "I promise to not mess with any paperboy or mailman; however, are you sure they are not wanting to play fetch?"

Who is Mr. Tay Tay?

Mr. Dain Taylor, an educator from Indiana, has a gift for writing and expressing himself. He has been blessed to serve Kitley for four years.

Mr. Taylor discovered his talent for writing two years ago while composing poems for his parents (Diane and Alfred Taylor) on Mother's Day and Father's Day. Dain holds a Bachelor's Degree in Spanish from Ball State University, is a licensed teacher from kindergarten to sixth grade, and has eight years of teaching experience as an instructional teaching assistant. Mr. Taylor also is a proud graduate of Indiana Wesleyan University, and has plans to publish other poems in the near future.

Interview with Nikki

Canine Interviewer: "Yes, we are here at the Taylor household at 212 North Vine Street with Nicolette Canine Taylor, also known as Nikki. Nikki, can you tell us a little bit more about yourself? What kind of dog are you? What are you like? What's your relationship with your master, Mr. Tay Tay?"

Nikki: "Well, my name is Nikki. I am a whippet, and I am the star of the book, Nikki's World: The Dog Walk."

Nikki: "I would say that my relationship with Mr. Tay Tay is complicated. I am a dog. He is a human being. He speaks English. I speak Caninese. Despite the language barrier, I would say the relationship is fair. I bark; he comes. I jump on him. He gives me a dog walk. We come back in from the dog walk; he gives me a snack. As any canine can observe, I am the ruler of this household."

Canine Interviewer: "What do you like to do? What are your interests and hobbies?"

Nikki: "I like to run around the house, sleep in my masters' beds, chase Atlas, eat kitty litter, be the center of attention, and cause chaos."

Canine Interviewer: "It has been a pleasure having you, Nikki, here with us. Canine and feline viewers all over the globe, thank you for tuning in with us. Join us next time with our feline friend, Atlas."

www.ingramcontent.com/pod-product-compliance
Lightning Source LLC
Chambersburg PA
CBRC102059150426
43193CB00006B/63